April 28, 2017

FEDERAL RESERVE SYSTEM

Simmons First National Corporation
Pine Bluff, Arkansas

Order Approving the Merger of Bank Holding Companies

Simmons First National Corporation ("Simmons"), Pine Bluff, Arkansas, a financial holding company within the meaning of the Bank Holding Company Act of 1956 ("BHC Act"),[1] has requested the Board's approval under section 3 of the BHC Act[2] to merge with Hardeman County Investment Company, Inc. ("Hardeman"), and thereby indirectly acquire First South Bank, both of Jackson, Tennessee.

Notice of the proposal, affording interested persons an opportunity to submit comments, has been published (81 Federal Register 86714 (December 1, 2016)).[3] The time for submitting comments has expired, and the Board has considered the proposal and all comments received in light of the factors set forth in section 3 of the BHC Act.

Simmons, with consolidated assets of approximately $8.4 billion, is the 147th largest insured depository organization in the United States. Simmons controls approximately $6.7 billion in consolidated deposits, which represent less than 1 percent of the total amount of deposits of insured depository institutions in the United States.[4] Simmons controls Simmons Bank, Pine Bluff, Arkansas, which operates in Arkansas, Kansas, Missouri, and Tennessee. Simmons is the 12th largest insured depository

---

[1] 12 U.S.C. § 1841 et seq.

[2] 12 U.S.C. § 1842.

[3] 12 CFR 262.3(b).

[4] National asset and deposit data are as of December 31, 2016, unless otherwise noted.

organization in Tennessee, controlling deposits of approximately $1.9 billion in Tennessee, which represent 1.4 percent of the total deposits of insured depository institutions in that state.[5]

Hardeman, with consolidated assets of approximately $477.4 million, is the 1463rd largest insured depository organization in the United States, controlling approximately $396.3 million in consolidated deposits, which represent less than 1 percent of the total amount of deposits of insured depository institutions in the United States. Hardeman controls First South Bank, which operates only in Tennessee. Hardeman is the 54th largest insured depository organization in Tennessee, controlling deposits of approximately $379.4 million, which represent less than 0.3 percent of the total deposits of insured depository institutions in that state.

On consummation of this proposal, Simmons would become the 140th largest insured depository organization in the United States, with consolidated assets of approximately $8.9 billion, which represent less than 1 percent of the total assets of insured depository institutions in the United States. Simmons would control consolidated deposits of approximately $7.1 billion, which represent less than 1 percent of the total amount of deposits of insured depository institutions in the United States. In Tennessee, Simmons would become the 9th largest insured depository organization, controlling deposits of approximately $2.3 billion in Tennessee, which represent 1.7 percent of the total deposits of insured depository institutions in that state.

Interstate and Deposit Cap Analysis

Section 3(d) of the BHC Act generally provides that, if certain conditions are met, the Board may approve an application by a bank holding company to acquire control of a bank located in a state other than the home state of the bank holding

---

[5] State deposit data are as of June 30, 2016. In this context, insured depository institutions include commercial banks, credit unions, savings associations, and savings banks.

company without regard to whether the transaction is prohibited under state law.[6] Under this section, the Board may not approve an application that would permit an out-of-state bank holding company to acquire a bank in a host state if the bank has not been in existence for the lesser of the state statutory minimum period of time or five years.[7] In addition, the Board may not approve an interstate application if the bank holding company controls, or would upon consummation of the proposed transaction control, more than 10 percent of the total deposits of insured depository institutions in the United States or, in certain circumstances, if the bank holding company would upon consummation control 30 percent or more of the total deposits of insured depository institutions in any state in which the acquirer and target have overlapping banking operations.[8]

For purposes of the BHC Act, the home state of Simmons is Arkansas, and the home state of First South Bank is Tennessee.[9] Simmons is well capitalized and well managed under applicable law, and Simmons Bank has a "Satisfactory" rating under the Community Reinvestment Act of 1977 ("CRA").[10] Tennessee has a three-year minimum age requirement, and First South Bank has been in existence for more than three years.[11]

---

[6] 12 U.S.C. § 1842(d)(1)(A).

[7] 12 U.S.C. § 1842(d)(1)(B).

[8] 12 U.S.C. § 1842(d)(2)(A) and (B). The acquiring and target institutions have overlapping banking operations in any state in which any bank to be acquired is located and the acquiring bank holding company controls any insured depository institution or a branch. For purposes of section 3(d) of the BHC Act, the Board considers a bank to be located in the states in which the bank is chartered or headquartered or operates a branch. See 12 U.S.C. § 1841(o)(4)–(7).

[9] See 12 U.S.C. § 1841(o)(4). A bank holding company's home state is the state in which the total deposits of all banking subsidiaries of such company were the largest on July 1, 1966, or the date on which the company became a bank holding company, whichever is later. A state bank's home state is the state in which the bank is chartered.

[10] 12 U.S.C. § 2901 et seq.

[11] See Tenn. Code Ann. § 45-2-1403(a).

On consummation of the proposed transaction, Simmons would control less than 1 percent of the total amount of consolidated deposits in insured depository institutions in the United States. Tennessee imposes a 30 percent limit on the total amount of in-state deposits that a single banking organization may control.[12] The combined organization would control approximately 1.7 percent of the total amount of deposits of insured depository institutions in Tennessee, the only state in which Simmons and Hardeman have overlapping banking operations. The Board has considered all other requirements under section 3(d) of the BHC Act, including Simmons's record of meeting the credit needs of the communities it serves. Accordingly, in light of all the facts of record, the Board may approve the proposal under section 3(d) of the BHC Act.

Competitive Considerations

Section 3 of the BHC Act prohibits the Board from approving a proposal that would result in a monopoly or would be in furtherance of an attempt to monopolize the business of banking in any relevant market. The BHC Act also prohibits the Board from approving a proposal that would substantially lessen competition or tend to create a monopoly in any banking market, unless the anticompetitive effects of the proposal are clearly outweighed in the public interest by the probable effect of the proposal in meeting the convenience and needs of the communities to be served.[13]

Simmons and Hardeman have subsidiary depository institutions that compete directly in the Dyersburg, Tennessee, banking market ("Dyersburg market"), the Jackson, Tennessee, banking market ("Jackson market"), and the Memphis, Tennessee, banking market ("Memphis market").[14] The Board has considered the competitive

---

[12] See Tenn. Code Ann. § 45-2-1404.

[13] 12 U.S.C. § 1842(c)(1).

[14] The Dyersburg market is defined as Dyer and Lake counties, both of Tennessee. The Jackson market is defined as Chester, Crockett, Gibson, Haywood, Madison, and Henderson (minus District 7) counties, all of Tennessee. The Memphis market is defined as Fayette, Shelby, and Tipton counties, all of Tennessee; city of Grand Junction in Hardeman County, Tennessee; Crittenden County, Arkansas; Benton, De Soto, Marshall,

effects of the proposal in these banking markets in light of all the facts of record. In particular, the Board has considered the number of competitors that would remain in the markets; the relative shares of total deposits in insured depository institutions in the markets ("market deposits") that Simmons would control;[15] the concentration levels of market deposits and the increase in these levels, as measured by the Herfindahl-Hirschman Index ("HHI") under the Department of Justice Bank Merger Competitive Review guidelines ("DOJ Bank Merger Guidelines");[16] and other characteristics of the markets.

Consummation of the proposal would be consistent with Board precedent and within the thresholds in the DOJ Bank Merger Guidelines for the Dyersburg,

---

Tate, and Tunica counties, all of Mississippi; the northern part of Coahoma County, Mississippi (including the cities of Friars Point, Coahoma, Lula, and Jonestown); Panola County, Mississippi (north of State Route 315 east to Sardis Lake, including the city of Sardis); and Quitman County, Mississippi (north of State Route 315, including the cities of Birdie and Sledge).

[15] Deposit and market share data are as of June 30, 2016, and unless otherwise noted, are based on calculations in which the deposits of thrift institutions are included at 50 percent. The Board previously has indicated that thrift institutions have become, or have the potential to become, significant competitors to commercial banks. See, e.g., Midwest Financial Group, 75 Federal Reserve Bulletin 386 (1989); National City Corporation, 70 Federal Reserve Bulletin 743 (1984). Thus, the Board regularly has included thrift deposits in the market share calculation on a 50 percent weighted basis. See, e.g., First Hawaiian, Inc., 77 Federal Reserve Bulletin 52 (1991).

[16] Under the DOJ Bank Merger Guidelines, a market is considered unconcentrated if the post-merger HHI is under 1000, moderately concentrated if the post-merger HHI is between 1000 and 1800, and highly concentrated if the post-merger HHI exceeds 1800. The Department of Justice ("DOJ") has informed the Board that a bank merger or acquisition generally would not be challenged (in the absence of other factors indicating anticompetitive effects) unless the post-merger HHI is at least 1800 and the merger increases the HHI by more than 200 points. Although the DOJ and the Federal Trade Commission issued revised Horizontal Merger Guidelines in 2010, the DOJ has confirmed that its Bank Merger Guidelines, which were issued in 1995, were not modified. See Press Release, Department of Justice (August 19, 2010), available at www.justice.gov/opa/pr/2010/August/10-at-938.html.

Jackson, and Memphis markets. Although the Dyersburg market would remain highly concentrated on consummation of the proposal, the increase in the HHI would not be large (91 points). Simmons would become the third largest depository organization in the market, with a market share only about 4 percentage points higher than Hardeman, which is the third largest depository organization prior to consummation of the proposal. Five competitors would remain in the market, including two depository organizations with a higher market share than Simmons. The largest depository organization in the market would control over 50 percent of market deposits.

On consummation of the proposal, the Jackson and Memphis markets would remain moderately concentrated, as measured by the HHI. Numerous competitors would remain in the Jackson and Memphis markets.[17]

---

[17] Simmons operates the 5th largest depository institution in the Dyersburg market, controlling approximately $30.3 million in deposits, which represent approximately 4.3 percent of market deposits. Hardeman operates the 3rd largest depository institution in the same market, controlling approximately $75.3 million in deposits, which represent approximately 10.6 percent of market deposits. On consummation of the proposed transaction, Simmons would become the 3rd largest depository institution in the market, controlling deposits of approximately $105.6 million, which represent approximately 15 percent of market deposits. The HHI for the Dyersburg market would increase by 91 points to 3934, and 5 competitors would remain in the market.

Simmons operates the 5th largest depository institution in the Jackson market, controlling approximately $274.0 million in deposits, which represent approximately 8 percent of market deposits. Hardeman operates the 7th largest depository institution in the same market, controlling approximately $191.5 million in deposits, which represent approximately 5 percent of market deposits. On consummation of the proposed transaction, Simmons would become the 3rd largest depository institution in the market, controlling deposits of approximately $465.6 million, which represent approximately 13 percent of market deposits. The HHI for the Jackson market would increase by 80 points to 1066, and 23 competitors would remain in the market.

Simmons operates the 40th largest depository institution in the Memphis market, controlling approximately $77.8 million in deposits, which represent less than 1 percent of market deposits. Hardeman operates the 53rd largest depository institution in the same market, controlling approximately $11.5 million in deposits, which represent less than 1 percent of market deposits. On consummation of the proposed transaction, Simmons would become the 37th largest depository institution in the market, controlling deposits of

The DOJ also has conducted a review of the potential competitive effects of the proposal and has advised the Board that consummation of the proposal would not likely have a significantly adverse effect on competition in any relevant banking market, including the Dyersburg, Jackson, and Memphis markets. In addition, the appropriate banking agencies have been afforded an opportunity to comment and have not objected to the proposal.

Based on all of the facts of record, the Board concludes that consummation of the proposal would not have a significantly adverse effect on competition or on the concentration of resources in the Dyersburg, Jackson, or Memphis banking markets or in any other relevant banking market. Accordingly, the Board determines that competitive considerations are consistent with approval.

Financial, Managerial, and Other Supervisory Considerations

In reviewing a proposal under section 3 of the BHC Act, the Board considers the financial and managerial resources and the future prospects of the institutions involved. In its evaluation of the financial factors, the Board reviews information regarding the financial condition of the organizations involved on both parent-only and consolidated bases, as well as information regarding the financial condition of the subsidiary depository institutions and the organizations' significant nonbanking operations. In this evaluation, the Board considers a variety of information including capital adequacy, asset quality, and earnings performance, as well as public comments on the proposal. The Board evaluates the financial condition of the combined organization, including its capital position, asset quality, liquidity, earnings prospects, and the impact of the proposed funding of the transaction. The Board also considers the ability of the organization to absorb the costs of the proposal and to complete effectively the proposed integration of the operations of the institutions. In assessing financial

---

approximately $89.3 million, which represent less than 1 percent of market deposits. The HHI for the Memphis market would increase by less than one point, and 57 competitors would remain in the market.

factors, the Board considers capital adequacy to be especially important. The Board considers the future prospects of the organizations involved in the proposal in light of their financial and managerial resources and the proposed business plan.

Simmons and Hardeman are both well capitalized, and the combined entity would remain so on consummation of the proposed transaction. The proposed transaction is a bank holding company merger that is structured as a cash and share exchange.[18] The asset quality, earnings, and liquidity of Simmons Bank and First South Bank are consistent with approval, and Simmons appears to have adequate resources to absorb the costs of the proposal and to complete the integration of the institutions' operations. In addition, future prospects are considered consistent with approval.

The Board also has considered the managerial resources of the organizations involved and of the proposed combined organization. The Board has reviewed the examination records of Simmons, Hardeman, and their subsidiary depository institutions, including assessments of their management, risk-management systems, and operations. In addition, the Board has considered information provided by Simmons; the Board's supervisory experiences and those of other relevant bank supervisory agencies with the organizations; and the organizations' records of compliance with applicable banking, consumer protection, and anti-money-laundering laws; as well as information provided by the commenter.

Simmons, Hardeman, and their subsidiary depository institutions are each considered to be well managed. Simmons has a record of successfully integrating organizations into its operations and risk-management systems after acquisitions. Simmons's directors and senior executive officers have knowledge of and experience in the banking and financial services sectors, and Simmons's risk-management program appears consistent with approval of this expansionary proposal.

---

[18] At the time of the merger, each share of Hardeman common stock would be converted into the right to receive cash and Simmons common stock based on an exchange ratio. Simmons has the financial resources to fund the transaction.

The Board also has considered Simmons's plans for implementing the proposal.[19] Simmons has conducted comprehensive due diligence and is devoting significant financial and other resources to address all aspects of the post-integration process for this proposal. Simmons does not anticipate making significant changes to its existing risk-management policies, procedures, and controls. These are considered acceptable from a supervisory perspective and would be implemented at the combined organization. In addition, Simmons's and Hardeman's management have the experience and resources to operate the combined organization in a safe and sound manner, and Simmons plans to integrate Hardeman's existing management and personnel in a manner that augments Simmons's management.[20]

Based on all the facts of record, including Simmons's supervisory record, managerial and operational resources, plans for operating the combined institution after consummation, and public comments on the proposal,[21] the Board concludes that considerations relating to the financial and managerial resources and future prospects of the organizations involved in the proposal, as well as the records of effectiveness of Simmons and Hardeman in combatting money-laundering activities, are consistent with approval.

---

[19] Simmons plans to operate First South Bank as a separate entity for an interim period following consummation of the holding company merger. After the interim period, Simmons anticipates merging First South Bank with and into Simmons Bank.

[20] On consummation, four individuals currently serving as senior management officials at Hardeman or First South Bank will serve as senior management officials at the Simmons banking organization. These individuals include Hardeman's current president and chief executive officer, who will be retained as the Jackson community chairman of Simmons Bank.

[21] A commenter questioned how Simmons plans to reduce Hardeman's annual non-interest expenses upon consummation of the proposal. As explained above, the Board considered Simmons's plans for operating the combined organization upon consummation and determined that those plans would not present financial, managerial, or safety and soundness concerns.

Convenience and Needs Considerations

In acting on a proposal under section 3 of the BHC Act, the Board considers the effects of the proposal on the convenience and needs of the communities to be served.[22] In its evaluation of the effects of the proposal on the convenience and needs of the communities to be served, the Board considers whether the relevant institutions are helping to meet the credit needs of the communities they serve, as well as other potential effects of the proposal on the convenience and needs of the communities to be served. In this evaluation, the Board places particular emphasis on the records of the relevant depository institutions under the CRA. The CRA requires the federal financial supervisory agencies to encourage insured depository institutions to help meet the credit needs of the local communities in which they operate, consistent with their safe and sound operation,[23] and requires the appropriate federal financial supervisory agency to assess a depository institution's record of helping to meet the credit needs of its entire community, including low- and moderate-income ("LMI") neighborhoods, in evaluating bank expansionary proposals.[24]

In addition, the Board considers the banks' overall compliance records and recent fair lending examinations. Fair lending laws require all lending institutions to provide applicants with equal access to credit, regardless of their race, ethnicity, or certain other characteristics. The Board also considers assessments of other relevant supervisors, the supervisory views of examiners, other supervisory information, information provided by the applicant, and comments received on the proposal. The Board also may consider the institution's business model, its marketing and outreach plans, the organization's plans after consummation, and any other information the Board deems relevant.

---

[22] 12 U.S.C. § 1842(c)(2).

[23] 12 U.S.C. § 2901(b).

[24] 12 U.S.C. § 2903.

In assessing the convenience and needs factor in this case, the Board has considered all the facts of record, including reports of examination of the CRA performance of Simmons Bank and First South Bank, the fair lending and compliance records of both banks, the supervisory views of the Federal Deposit Insurance Corporation ("FDIC") and the Office of the Comptroller of the Currency ("OCC"), confidential supervisory information, information provided by Simmons, and the public comments received on the proposal.

Summary of Public Comments on Convenience and Needs

In this case, the Board received comments from a commenter objecting to the proposal on the basis of alleged disparities in the rates at which Simmons denied applications for conventional home purchase loans by Africans Americans, as compared to whites, in the Little Rock, Arkansas, Metropolitan Statistical Area ("Little Rock MSA") and the Memphis, Tennessee-Mississippi-Arkansas, Metropolitan Statistical Area ("Memphis MSA"), as reflected in data reported under the Home Mortgage Disclosure Act ("HMDA") for 2015. In addition, the commenter alleged that Simmons's HMDA reporting record is not credible and does not accurately reflect its loan denial rates.[25]

Businesses of the Involved Institutions and Response to Comments

Simmons Bank offers a broad range of retail and commercial banking products to consumers and businesses. Through its network of branches across Arkansas, Kansas, Missouri, and Tennessee, the bank offers a variety of banking products including commercial, residential, agricultural, and consumer loans, personal checking and savings accounts, business checking and savings accounts, money market accounts, cash

---

[25] The commenter also cited an anonymous customer complaint posted to a public online forum in 2015 that alleged problems with Simmons Bank's overdraft and return policies and expressed concern over the fees that were allegedly charged by the bank on the customer's account. As part of its review of this proposal, the Board considered information collected by the Federal Reserve Bank of St. Louis regarding the customer complaint and Simmons Bank's overdraft and return fee programs.

management products and services, credit cards, merchant services, and wealth management services.

First South Bank offers a more limited range of retail and commercial products through 10 branches in Tennessee, including deposit and loan products, debit cards, mobile phone banking, bill pay, and internet banking.

In response to the comments, Simmons represents that its HMDA and CRA data integrity are regularly verified through internal auditing reviews and regulatory examinations, and that regulatory compliance is an integral component of Simmons Bank's operating plan. Simmons also represents that an analysis of Simmons Bank's geographic and demographic lending activity is performed at least once annually and Simmons Bank retains appropriate documentation relating to its CRA program.

In addition, Simmons argues that the 2015 HMDA data referenced by the commenter does not fairly represent Simmons Bank's lending activities in the Little Rock MSA and the Memphis MSA, and that the bank's lending is fully compliant with all applicable CRA and fair lending requirements. Simmons asserts that the denial rates referenced by the commenter reflect determinations based on an applicant's credit history, debt-to-income ratios, insufficient collateral, and other nondiscriminatory factors. Simmons asserts that the bank continues to enhance its CRA program by increasing its marketing efforts toward LMI borrowers and developing more lending products, such as the Affordable Advantage Mortgage program (the "Mortgage Program"). The Mortgage Program, designed by Simmons Bank in 2015, has flexible qualifying and underwriting guidelines that target LMI census tracts and LMI borrowers, including those in the Little Rock and Memphis MSAs.

Simmons states that, in the Little Rock MSA, it has significantly increased its conventional home purchase lending to African Americans from 2015 to 2016, as reflected in Simmons Bank's 2016 HMDA data. Simmons represents that the number of conventional home purchase loan applications received and originated from African Americans during the 2016 HMDA review period increased substantially, as compared to the prior year. Simmons attributes these increases to the Mortgage Program, which it began offering in certain markets in 2015. Simmons represents that the Mortgage Program features flexible qualifying and underwriting guidelines and is specifically designed to increase the bank's home purchase and home refinance lending to LMI borrowers and communities.

In the Memphis MSA, Simmons asserts that disparities in Simmons Bank's lending record to African Americans, as reflected in 2015 HMDA data, are attributable to the bank entering the MSA in 2015 through an acquisition. As a result, Simmons asserts that it had a limited presence in the MSA during the 2015 HMDA review period and received few conventional home purchase loan applications from African Americans. However, Simmons represents that it has since taken steps to increase its lending to LMI and minority borrowers by extending the availability of its Mortgage Program to the Memphis MSA.

As part of Simmons's efforts to continue to enhance its CRA program, Simmons represents that it has established lending benchmarks for its full-scope and limited-scope markets, including community development lending benchmarks, and diversified investment goals and community development service goals at the branch level. To assist in the marketing of its products to LMI borrowers, Simmons represents that it has employed CRA mortgage lenders in the Little Rock and Memphis MSAs.

Records of Performance Under the CRA

In evaluating the convenience and needs factor and CRA performance, the Board considers substantial information in addition to information provided by public commenters and the applicant's response to the comments. In particular, the Board evaluates an institution's performance record in light of examinations by the appropriate federal supervisors of the CRA performance records of the relevant institutions, as well as information and views provided by the appropriate federal supervisors.[26] In this case,

---

[26] See Interagency Questions and Answers Regarding Community Reinvestment, 81 Federal Register 48506, 48548 (July 25, 2016).

the Board considered the supervisory views of its supervisory staff and of examiners from the Federal Reserve Bank of St. Louis ("Reserve Bank"), the FDIC, and the OCC.

The CRA requires that the appropriate federal financial supervisor for a depository institution prepare a written evaluation of the institution's record of helping to meet the credit needs of its entire community, including LMI neighborhoods.[27] An institution's most recent CRA performance evaluation is a particularly important consideration in the applications process because it represents a detailed, on-site evaluation by the institution's primary federal supervisor of the institution's overall record of lending in its communities.

In general, federal financial supervisors apply lending, investment, and service tests to evaluate the performance of a large insured depository institution in helping to meet the credit needs of the communities it serves. The lending test specifically evaluates the institution's home mortgage, small business, small farm, and community development lending to determine whether the institution is helping to meet the credit needs of individuals and geographies of all income levels. As part of the lending test, examiners review and analyze an institution's data reported under HMDA, in addition to small business, small farm, and community development loan data collected and reported under the CRA regulations, to assess an institution's lending activities with respect to borrowers and geographies of different income levels. The institution's lending performance is based on a variety of factors, including (1) the number and amounts of home mortgage, small business, small farm, and consumer loans (as applicable) in the institution's assessment areas; (2) the geographic distribution of the institution's lending in its assessment areas and the number and amounts of loans in low-, moderate-, middle-, and upper-income geographies; (3) the distribution of loans based on borrower characteristics, including, for home mortgage loans, the number and amounts of

---

[27] 12 U.S.C. § 2906.

loans to low-, moderate-, middle-, and upper-income individuals;[28] (4) the institution's community development lending, including the number and amounts of community development loans and their complexity and innovativeness; and (5) the institution's use of innovative or flexible lending practices to address the credit needs of LMI individuals and geographies.

The Board is concerned when HMDA data reflect disparities in the rates of loan applications, originations, and denials among members of different racial or ethnic groups in local areas. These types of disparities may indicate weaknesses in the adequacy of policies and programs at an institution for meeting its obligations to extend credit fairly. However, other information critical to an institution's credit decisions is not available from HMDA data.[29] Consequently, HMDA data disparities must be evaluated in the context of other information regarding the lending record of an institution.

CRA Performance of Simmons Bank

Simmons Bank was assigned an overall rating of "Satisfactory" at its most recent CRA performance evaluation by the OCC, as of January 2, 2013 ("Simmons Bank

---

[28] Examiners also consider the number and amounts of small business and small farm loans to businesses and farms with gross annual revenues of $1 million or less, small business and small farm loans by loan amount at origination, and consumer loans, if applicable, to low-, moderate-, middle-, and upper-income individuals. See, e.g., 12 CFR 228.22(b)(3).

[29] Other data relevant to credit decisions could include credit history, debt-to-income ratios, and loan-to-value ratios. Accordingly, when conducting fair lending examinations, examiners analyze such additional information before reaching a determination regarding an institution's compliance with fair lending laws.

Evaluation").[30] The bank received "Low Satisfactory" ratings for both the Lending Test and Investment Test and a "High Satisfactory" rating for the Service Test.[31]

Examiners found that Simmons Bank's overall lending levels reflected adequate responsiveness to credit needs in its assessment areas. According to examiners, the bank originated a substantial majority of loans within its assessment areas, and the distribution of its loans across income levels and businesses of different sizes was adequate. In particular, examiners found that the bank's overall distribution of home mortgage loans to geographies of different income levels was adequate.

In Arkansas, Simmons Bank's performance under the Lending Test was rated "Low Satisfactory." Examiners found that the bank's overall geographic distribution of home mortgage loans was adequate, and its overall geographic distribution of small loans to businesses and farms was good. The bank was found to offer flexible loan programs, including for home mortgage and farm loans. In the Little Rock MSA, an area of concern for the commenter, the bank's lending volume was considered adequate.

With respect to the Investment Test, examiners found that Simmons Bank had an overall adequate level of qualified investments based on the investment opportunities and dollar volume of investments made in its assessment areas. In Arkansas, the bank received a "Low Satisfactory" rating for the Investment Test. In the

---

[30] The Simmons Bank Evaluation was conducted using Large Institution CRA Examination Procedures. The examiners reviewed home purchase, home improvement, and home refinance mortgage loans reported pursuant to the HMDA, and small loans made to businesses and farms reported under CRA data-collection requirements, for 2009 through 2011. The evaluation period for community development lending, investments, and services was September 30, 2008, through January 2, 2013.

[31] The Simmons Bank Evaluation included full-scope evaluations of the Fort Smith, Arkansas-Oklahoma Multistate MSA; the Little Rock-North Little Rock, Arkansas MSA; the Pine Bluff, Arkansas MSA; non-Metropolitan Arkansas (comprised of Searcy, Stone, and Van Buren counties); the Kansas City, Kansas-Missouri Multistate MSA; the Wichita, Kansas MSA; and the Springfield, Missouri MSA. Limited-scope evaluations were performed in Fulton and Sharp counties, both of Arkansas, and Saline County of Kansas.

Little Rock MSA, examiners concluded that the bank's level of qualified investments was poor.

As noted, Simmons Bank received a "High Satisfactory" rating for the Service Test. Examiners found the bank's delivery systems to be accessible to all sections of its assessment areas, including to individuals of different income levels. Examiners noted that, overall, the bank provided a good level of community development services in the areas in which the bank maintained an ongoing presence, including by providing technical assistance to programs that support affordable housing, small businesses, and economic development in LMI geographies.

In Arkansas, Simmons Bank received a "High Satisfactory" rating for the Service Test. Examiners noted that the bank's retail branch distribution in Arkansas was good and that the bank provided a good level of community development services. In the Little Rock MSA, examiners found the bank's branch delivery systems to be adequate and reasonably accessible to geographies and individuals of different income levels.

Simmons Bank's Efforts since the Simmons Bank Evaluation

Simmons represents that, since the Simmons Bank Evaluation, Simmons Bank has made significant efforts to enhance its ability to serve the credit needs of the communities it serves. These efforts include hiring a full-time, experienced, CRA officer, completing two self-assessment examinations, offering a wider variety of Small Business Administration loans, and enhancing its CRA performance monitoring compliance systems. In addition, Simmons notes that it created a Community Development Department and established a CRA Strategic Plan in 2014 to better address its expanding CRA obligations.

The CRA Strategic Plan applies to all markets in which Simmons Bank operates, including the Little Rock and Memphis MSAs. Simmons represents that it reviews and revises its CRA Strategic Plan annually to reflect the bank's expanding line of financial products as well as the increased number of deposit and loan products being offered by Simmons within its markets. For example, Simmons notes that in 2015 it created internal CRA performance benchmarks and in 2016 it enhanced the bank's CRA goals by establishing specific lending benchmarks, community development lending benchmarks, a diversified investment goal, and community development services goals at the branch level.

In addition, Simmons represents that it has established community advisory committees across Arkansas, Tennessee, and Missouri. These committees are comprised of LMI service providers that represent a variety of groups, including public housing authorities and non-profit organizations. Simmons further represents that these advisory committees provide it with an additional platform to identify ways to serve the communities in which Simmons serves.

In the Little Rock MSA, Simmons represents that it has expanded its CRA activities as part of broader improvements to its CRA program. Simmons further represents that its employees actively support a variety of community development initiatives in the Little Rock MSA, including through efforts to promote affordable housing, community economic development, and financial literacy. Furthermore, Simmons notes that, in 2015 and 2016, Simmons Bank provided several grants to support affordable housing initiatives in the Little Rock MSA. With respect to the Memphis MSA, Simmons notes that it entered the market in 2015 through an acquisition and first developed CRA performance goals for the market in 2016. These initiatives include developing an affordable home-improvement mortgage product that will be marketed to communities in Memphis and providing financial literacy training to small businesses. Simmons states that it expects to continue its existing CRA activities in the Little Rock and Memphis MSAs after consummation of the proposal. Simmons notes that it continues to evaluate its marketing activities in an effort to identify more effective ways to reach LMI individuals and communities.

CRA Performance of First South Bank

First South Bank received an overall rating of "Satisfactory" at its most recent CRA performance evaluation by the FDIC, as of September 12, 2016 ("First South

Bank Evaluation"),[32] with ratings of "Satisfactory" for the Lending Test and "Outstanding" for the Community Development Test.[33]

Examiners concluded that First South Bank exhibited a satisfactory overall record with respect to the Lending Test. Examiners noted that a majority of the bank's small business and home mortgage loans, by number and dollar volume, were made in its assessment areas. Examiners found that the distribution of the bank's borrowers reflected reasonable penetration among individuals of different income levels and businesses of different sizes, and the geographic distribution of its loans reflected reasonable dispersion for the bank as a whole.

In addition, examiners concluded that First South Bank demonstrated excellent responsiveness to community development needs in its assessment areas through a combination of community development loans, qualified investments, and community development services. Examiners found that the bank's community development loans demonstrated adequate responsiveness to the community development needs of its assessment areas. In addition, examiners found that the bank demonstrated an excellent record of making qualified investments, as reflected in the relative volume of its investments and the responsiveness of those investments in meeting community development needs. Examiners also found that the bank provided an excellent level of community development services relative to its resources, including to community organizations that primarily provide services to LMI individuals. Examiners noted that First South Bank maintained banking hours and services that are typical for the industry

---

[32] The First South Bank Evaluation was conducted using the Interagency Intermediate Small Institution Examination Procedures. Examiners reviewed small business loans from the 2015 calendar year. Examiners reviewed home mortgage loans reported pursuant to HMDA data-collection requirements (geographic distribution and borrower distribution) from 2014 through June 30, 2016. The evaluation period for community development loans, investments, and services was from March 4, 2014, through September 12, 2016.

[33] The First South Bank Evaluation included a full-scope evaluation of the Madison County assessment area in the Jackson, Tennessee MSA, and a limited-scope evaluation of the Tennessee Non-MSA (consisting of Dyer, Hardeman, and Haywood counties).

and areas that it serves. In addition, the bank offered alternative delivery systems such as mobile and online banking.

Additional Supervisory Views

In 2016, Simmons Bank changed from a national bank to a state member bank, resulting in the Reserve Bank becoming the bank's primary supervisor. As part of Simmons Bank's conversion, the Reserve Bank carried out a pre-membership examination. Since Simmons Bank became a state member bank, the Reserve Bank has performed targeted exams of the bank's consumer compliance program. The Board has considered the results of these examinations as well as Simmons Bank's record of complying with fair lending and other consumer protection laws.

Additional Convenience and Needs Considerations

The Board also considers other potential effects of the proposal on the convenience and needs of the communities to be served. Simmons represents that it plans to continue its current offering of products and services after consummation of the proposal. In addition, Simmons represents that it plans to operate First South Bank as a separate entity for an interim period of time prior to scheduling the merger of First South Bank with and into Simmons Bank. During the interim period, Simmons anticipates that both banks would continue to offer their legacy products and services. Simmons notes that customers of First South Bank could be referred to branches of Simmons Bank for access to Simmons's broader offering of products and services. According to Simmons, such referrals could occur upon a customer's request or if a customer is identified as a candidate for products and services only offered by Simmons.

Upon completion of the bank merger and systems conversion, Simmons represents that its products and services would become available to customers of First South Bank at that bank's former locations. Simmons represents that many of these products and services have more flexible features than those currently offered by First South Bank. These include credit card products, signature guarantees, and Simmons Bank's "Positive Pay" anti-fraud account reconciliation service. In addition, Simmons asserts that customers of First South Bank would benefit from a more expansive branch and ATM network located across four states.

Conclusion on Convenience and Needs Considerations

The Board has considered all the facts of record, including the CRA records of the relevant depository institutions involved, the institutions' records of compliance with fair lending and other consumer protection laws, confidential supervisory information, information provided by Simmons, the public comments on the proposal, and other potential effects of the proposal on the convenience and needs of the communities to be served. Based on that review, the Board concludes that the convenience and needs factor is consistent with approval.

Financial Stability

The Dodd-Frank Wall Street Reform and Consumer Protection Act ("Dodd-Frank Act") amended section 3 of the BHC Act to require the Board to consider a proposal's risk "to the stability of the United States banking or financial system."[34]

To assess the likely effect of a proposed transaction on the stability of the U.S. banking or financial system, the Board considers a variety of metrics that capture the systemic "footprint" of the resulting firm and the incremental effect of the transaction on the systemic footprint of the acquiring firm. These metrics include measures of the size of the resulting firm, the availability of substitute providers for any critical products and services offered by the resulting firm, the interconnectedness of the resulting firm with the banking or financial system, the extent to which the resulting firm contributes to the complexity of the financial system, and the extent of the cross-border activities of the resulting firm.[35] These categories are not exhaustive, and additional categories could inform the Board's decision. In addition to these quantitative measures, the Board

---

[34] Section 604(d) of the Dodd-Frank Act, Pub. L. No. 111-203, 124 Stat. 1376, 1601 (2010), codified at 12 U.S.C. § 1842(c)(7).

[35] Many of the metrics considered by the Board measure an institution's activities relative to the U.S. financial system.

considers qualitative factors, such as the opaqueness and complexity of an institution's internal organization, that are indicative of the relative degree of difficulty of resolving the resulting firm. A financial institution that can be resolved in an orderly manner is less likely to inflict material damage to the broader economy.[36]

The Board's experience has shown that proposals involving an acquisition of less than $10 billion in assets, or that results in a firm with less than $100 billion in total assets, are generally not likely to pose systemic risks. Accordingly, the Board presumes that a proposal does not raise material financial stability concerns if the assets involved fall below either of these size thresholds, absent evidence that the transaction would result in a significant increase in interconnectedness, complexity, cross-border activities, or other risk factors.[37]

In this case, the Board has considered information relevant to risks to the stability of the U.S. banking or financial system. The proposal involves a target that has less than $10 billion in assets and a pro forma organization of less than $100 billion in assets. Both the acquirer and the target are predominantly engaged in a variety of retail commercial banking activities.[38] The pro forma organization would have minimal cross-border activities and would not exhibit an organizational structure, complex interrelationships, or unique characteristics that would complicate resolution of the firm in the event of financial distress. In addition, the organization would not be a critical

---

[36] For further discussion of the financial stability standard, see Capital One Financial Corporation, FRB Order No. 2012-2 (February 14, 2012).

[37] See People's United Financial, Inc., FRB Order No. 2017-08 at 25-26 (March 16, 2017). Notwithstanding this presumption, the Board has the authority to review the financial stability implications of any proposal. For example, an acquisition involving a global systemically important bank could warrant a financial stability review by the Board, regardless of the size of the acquisition.

[38] In each of the activities in which it engages, Simmons has, and as a result of the proposal would continue to have, a small market share on a nationwide basis, and numerous competitors would remain for these services.

services provider or so interconnected with other firms or the markets that it would pose a significant risk to the financial system in the event of financial distress.

In light of all the facts and circumstances, this transaction would not appear to result in meaningfully greater or more concentrated risks to the stability of the U.S. banking or financial system. Based on these and all other facts of record, the Board determines that considerations relating to financial stability are consistent with approval.

Conclusion

Based on the foregoing and all the facts of record, the Board determines that the proposal should be, and hereby is, approved.[39] In reaching its conclusion, the Board has considered all the facts of record in light of the factors that it is required to consider under the BHC Act and other applicable statutes. Approval of this proposal is specifically conditioned on compliance by Simmons with all the conditions set forth in this Order, including receipt of all required regulatory approvals, and on the commitments made to the Board in connection with the proposal. For purposes of this

---

[39] The commenter requested that the Board hold a public hearing or meeting on the proposal. Section 3(b) of the BHC Act does not require that the Board hold a public hearing on any application unless the appropriate supervisory authorities for the bank to be acquired make a timely written recommendation of denial of the application. 12 U.S.C. § 1842(b); 12 CFR 225.16(e). The Board has not received such a recommendation from the appropriate supervisory authorities. Under its rules, the Board also may, in its discretion, hold a public hearing if appropriate to allow interested persons an opportunity to provide relevant testimony when written comments would not adequately represent their views. The Board has considered the commenter's request in light of all the facts of record. In the Board's view, the commenter has had ample opportunity to submit comments on the proposal and, in fact, submitted written comments that the Board has considered in acting on the proposal. The commenter's request did not identify disputed issues of fact material to the Board's decision that would be clarified by a public meeting. In addition, the request did not demonstrate why written comments do not present the commenter's views adequately or why a hearing or meeting otherwise would be necessary or appropriate. For these reasons, and based on all the facts of record, the Board has determined that a public hearing or meeting is not required or warranted in this case. Accordingly, the request for a public hearing on the proposal is denied.

action, the conditions and commitments are deemed to be conditions imposed in writing by the Board in connection with its findings and decision herein and, as such, may be enforced in proceedings under applicable law.

The proposal may not be consummated before the fifteenth calendar day after the effective date of this Order, or later than three months thereafter, unless such period is extended for good cause by the Board or by the Reserve Bank, acting under delegated authority.

By order of the Board of Governors,[40] effective April 28, 2017.

Ann E. Misback (signed)
Ann E. Misback
Secretary of the Board

---

[40] Voting for this action: Chair Yellen, Vice Chairman Fischer, and Governors Powell and Brainard.

www.ingramcontent.com/pod-product-compliance
Lightning Source LLC
Chambersburg PA
CBHW081319180526
45170CB00007B/2772